STRANGE KICKS & BOUNCES

Funny, Whimsical, Legendary & True Tales of Golf

by the Editors of *Golf Magazine*

TRIUMPH
BOOKS
CHICAGO

Printed in China

Book design by Graffolio.

Cover design by Salvatore Concialdi.

Illustrations, including cover, by Richard Anderson.

This book is available in quantity at special discounts for your group or organization. For further information, contact:

> Triumph Books
> 644 South Clark Street
> Chicago, Illinois 60605
> (312) 939-3330

ISBN 1-57243-171-7

Contents

Fore Word

Each month an odd ritual takes place in the homes of many of the 1.3 million readers of *Golf Magazine*. When their issue arrives, they turn to the back page first.

Why? For more than a decade, the back page has been home to a compelling collection of facts, anecdotes, trivia, humor, and offbeat items from the world of golf — a collection we call "Out of Bounds."

As its name implies, "Out of Bounds" takes our readers beyond the markers, on a wide-ranging monthly journey to golf's outer limits. You never know quite what you'll find on the "Out of Bounds" page. You may learn which president added a green to the White House, or why Gene Sarazen wanted to enlarge the hole, or where free relief is allowed for hippo footprints. "Out of Bounds" is as quirky and unpredictable as the game of golf itself.

Typically, we can squeeze only a dozen or so of these gems into our monthly "Out of Bounds" page. But now, thanks to the book you're holding, you can sample from more than four hundred items — the "Best of Out of Bounds," if you will.

So enjoy the trip — and in this case, feel free to start on page one.

George Peper
Editor-in-Chief
Golf Magazine

"It's good sportsmanship to not pick up lost golf balls while they are still rolling."
— *Mark Twain*

*I*t's good sportsmanship to not pick up lost golf balls while they are still rolling.

— *Mark Twain*

I have a tip that can take five strokes off anyone's golf game. It's called an eraser.

— *Arnold Palmer*

*I*f you drink, don't drive. Don't even putt.

— *Dean Martin*

*M*ickey Mantle, the former New York Yankees outfielder, loved riding golf carts. "He who has fastest golf cart never have bad lie."

Mantle figured first to his ball would mean a good lie.

*L*ay off golf for three weeks, and then quit.

— *Sam Snead, advising a pupil*

*G*ive me golf clubs, fresh air, and a beautiful partner and you can keep the golf clubs and fresh air.

— *Jack Benny*

*J*ust figure out a way to get it in the hole, no matter what it looks like.

— *Lee Trevino*

*N*inety percent of the putts that fall short don't go in.

— *Yogi Berra*

The money is completely unimportant — once you have won enough of it.

— *Johnny Miller*

The best diet I know is pride in yourself. If I gain an inch on my waist, I have to send two hundred pairs of slacks out for alteration.

— *Doug Sanders*

If profanity had an influence on the flight of the ball, the game would be played far better than it is.

— *British writer Horace Hutchinson,*
Hints on the Game of Golf, 1886.

Every time I have the urge to play golf I lie down until the urge passes.

— *Humorist Sam Levenson*

Golf is a game whose aim is to hit a very small ball into an even smaller hole, with weapons singularly ill-designed for that purpose.

— *Winston Churchill*

Never bet with anyone you meet on the first tee who has a deep suntan, a 1-iron in his bag, and squinty eyes.

— *Dave Marr*

A man's true colors will surface quicker in a five-dollar Nassau than in any other form of peace-time diversion that I can name.

— *Grantland Rice*

2

*Mishaps &
Misfortunes*

*All the honking in the world couldn't get Seve Ballesteros
to the 1980 U.S. Open on time.*

$\mathcal{A}$ terrible traffic tie-up caused Seve Ballesteros to arrive late at the 1980 U.S. Open at Baltusrol Golf Club. Reaching the first tee moments after his playing companions hit their second shots onto the first green, the reigning British Open champion was disqualified.

$\mathcal{W}$hen world-traveler Greg Norman arrived in Spain for a tournament, he was greeted with a cool "adios" instead of a warmhearted "bien venido" and was promptly escorted to a plane bound for London. The problem? The Shark didn't have a visa. "I haven't been back to Spain since," he said.

*A*waiting the start of a qualifying round for the 1984 U.S. Open, Roger Maltbie rented a golf cart. Thinking the USGA had relaxed its normal ban against riding during events, Maltbie drove past an official on the first tee. By the time he drove past an official at the ninth hole, he had accrued twelve penalty shots.

*A*t a tournament in Sweden, Steve Elkington, winner of the 1991 Players Championship, plucked a piece of grass to chew on and was penalized two strokes for touching the ground in a hazard.

*I*n the 1971 Ryder Cup, Arnold Palmer hit a 5-iron to the par-three seventh green. An opponent's caddie, an American college student, gushed, "What a great shot, Mr. Palmer! What did you use?" Palmer told the caddie, and although the hole was halved with pars, officials later awarded it to the Americans due to illegally sought "advice" from the opposition.

*A*pproaching the final two holes of the 1939 U.S. Open, Sam Snead knew two pars would equal the championship record of 281, a score he thought would clinch the victory. Snead bogeyed the 71st hole and, thinking he needed a birdie on the finishing par five, gambled unnecessarily. The result: a disastrous eight. In reality, a bogey would have given Snead his only U.S. Open title.

*F*illing out his scorecard after a pro-am at Doral in 1970, Ray Floyd wrote his front-side total of 36 in the box reserved for the 9th hole. He signed the card, turned it in, and posted a round of 110.

*I*n the 1968 French Open, British pro Brian Barnes missed a short putt for par and then tried to rake the ball back into the cup. His backhand missed. So did his next forehand. Livid, he began batting the ball back and forth, once straddling the line, incurring a two-stroke penalty. He holed out for a 15.

*P*erhaps Wayne Grady needed his eyes checked, or maybe he wasn't paying attention. At the start of the 1987 season, the Australian was disqualified twice in five weeks for playing the wrong ball.

*H*arry Bradshaw led the 1949 British Open after the first day. In the second round, his drive at the fifth hole rolled into the broken shards of a discarded beer bottle. Unsure whether relief was available and wanting to avoid a delay, Bradshaw smashed the ball out, took a double bogey, and lost in a playoff to Bobby Locke two days later.

*A*fter Ben Crenshaw's ball lodged in a palm tree at Palm Springs in 1981, his caddie climbed onto a stepladder and shook the tree. About three dozen balls fell out. Crenshaw's was not among them.

*I*n early 1938, Ben Hogan, nearly penniless at the time, was playing an event in Oakland. The night before the final round, somebody stole the tires off his car. Hogan, in tears upon discovering the theft, declared, "I can't go another inch. I'm finished." Hogan shot a 69 the next day to finish second and earn $380 to keep him going.

*D*ick Mayer used an interesting tactic in winning the 1957 U.S. Open, his only major. In the playoff against slow-playing Cary Middlecoff, Mayer brought a stool with him around the course and sat down while Middlecoff painstakingly prepared to hit his shots. Middlecoff shot 79 while Mayer shot 72.

*I*n the final round of the 1889 British Open at Musselburgh, Andrew Kirkaldy's first putt on the 14th hole stopped one inch short of the cup. After making a one-handed stab that missed the ball altogether, he said, "If the hole were big enough, I'd bury myself in it." Kirkaldy lost in a playoff to Willie Park.

*Dick Mayer made himself comfortable during the final
round of the 1957 U.S. Open in which he beat the sluggish
Cary Middlecoff.*

*T*ommy Armour achieved dubious fame during the 1927 Shawnee (Pennsylvania) Open when he hooked ten balls out of bounds on the 17th hole, eventually carding a 23 — the highest one-hole score by a pro in a PGA Tour event. Armour had won the U.S. Open a week earlier.

*I*t looked as if Tommy Armour's highest one-hole score record would fall during the 1978 French Open at La Baule. French pro Philippe Porquier was 50 yards short of the green in two when he got a case of the "shanks" near a boundary fence. After depositing ball after ball out of bounds, he managed a 20 — the European record for highest one-hole score.

*I*n the third round of the 1921 British Open at St. Andrews, amateur Roger Wethered stepped on his ball while walking backward after studying his line on the 14th green. The one-stroke penalty cost him the championship, as he tied with Jock Hutchison and then lost the playoff.

*O*ften gamesmanship can get out of hand. While playing with Jimmy Demaret at the San Andres Country Club in Buenos Aires, Sam Snead rolled a long putt right up to the cup that would have dropped had it not rebounded a foot backward. Upon closer inspection, Snead noticed someone had planted toothpicks around the cup.

17

*T*he story is told at St. Andrews of a player who fluffed his approach shot at 18 into the Swilcan Burn. He picked up, dropped over his shoulder, and chipped into the burn again, picked up, dropped and chipped in a third time. He took his clubs from the caddie, threw them into the burn, threw his caddie in, and jumped in himself.

*R*oberto de Vicenzo inadvertently signed his scorecard posting a par instead of a birdie on the 17th hole at the 1968 Masters. This technical error gave him a score one stroke higher than he actually shot and gave the green jacket to Bob Goalby.

*F*olklore has it that after Jimmy Durante completed his first round ever — he scored well into the 200s — he asked his companions, "What should I give the caddie?" The answer: "Your clubs."

*T*he night before the 1974 Spanish Open, Seve Ballesteros, then seventeen, said it was "impossible" for a pro to score double figures on a hole at even par. His first drive hooked out of bounds, his second shot sliced out of bounds, his sixth shot found a lake and his eighth was in a bunker. On in nine, he putted in for 11.

$\mathcal{J}$ackie Pung had the lowest score at the 1957 U.S. Women's Open at Winged Foot, but lost the championship. Her signed scorecard showed a five on the fourth hole instead of the correct six, although the final round total of 72 was correct. She was disqualified. Members, officials, and spectators later collected $3,000 for her as consolation.

$\mathcal{B}$ill Garniss was playing the eighth hole at Bass River Golf Club, South Yarmouth, Massachusetts, when he hit a low 4-wood shot. The ball headed for a greenside bunker and stopped dead. Garniss found the ball impaled on the spike of the bunker rake.

Harry Leach was down in the dumps after his tee shot landed in a garbage lorry crossing the first fairway at St. Andrews.

*A*ccording to *The Golf Hall of Shame*, in 1954 Harry Leach hit what looked like a normal drive off the first tee at St. Andrews. That is until his ball landed in a garbage truck crossing the fairway. His drive stopped moving at the town dump a mile away.

*G*reg Norman's level of anxiety rose when the first two rounds of the 1983 Hong Kong Open were rained out. He found relief by driving one hundred golf balls through the open window of his hotel room into Hong Kong harbor. The practice paid off: Norman won what became a 36-hole event.

*A*rnold Palmer was seven shots off the lead in the 1960 U.S. Open at Cherry Hills when he hit his opening tee shot of the final round. That drive reached the green 346 yards away. Palmer birdied the hole on the way to a 65 and his only Open title.

*A*ccording to the *Guinness Book of World Records*, Kelly Robbins struck the longest recorded drive by a woman, 429.7 yards at the Elmira Corning Regional Airport in Corning, New York, on May 22, 1995.

*T*he longest tee shot ever may have been the ball hit at John O'Gaunt Club in England. It flew into a vegetable truck and didn't hit the ground until the truck was unloaded 40 miles away at Covent Garden in London.

*J*ohn Daly hit the longest hole in U.S. Open history in two monstrous shots during the second round of the 1993 Open. He tamed the 630-yard 17th on Baltusrol's Lower Course with a 321-yard drive and a 310-yard one-iron.

*O*ne of John Daly's biggest drives was hit during a practice round for the 1993 British Open at Royal St. George's. Daly drove the 431-yard, dogleg left fifth hole.

*T*he starter at the Eden course, St. Andrews, Scotland, once witnessed a visitor slice his tee shot as a northbound train was passing. The ball went through a window of the train and was thrown back immediately by a man in the car, who waved cheerfully to the golfer.

In 1962, Nils Lied, an Australian meteorologist stationed at Mawson Base, Antarctica, drove a golf ball a record 2,640 yards (1.5 miles) across a sheet of ice.

The longest recorded non-straight hole-in-one par five was made by Shaun Lynch. Shaun holed his tee shot on the 496-yard 17th hole at Teigh Valley Golf Club in Newton Abbott, England.

The longest straight hole ever aced is the 10th at the aptly named Miracle Hills Golf Club in Omaha. On October 7, 1965, Robert Mitera's tee shot found the cup 444 yards away.

*I*t's remarkable that Norman L. Manley made consecutive holes in one at Del Valle Country Club in California on September 2, 1964. What's unbelieveable is that the seventh and eighth holes are 330 and 220 yards long.

*B*efore the 1977 Lancome Tournament in Paris, Arnold Palmer drove off the second tier of the Eiffel Tower — 300 feet off the ground. The longest ball went 403 yards, while one of them hooked and hit a bus.

*C*raig Wood's 430-yard drive on the par-five fifth at St. Andrews during the 1933 British Open is thought to be the longest drive in major history. It didn't help Wood win — he lost in a playoff to Denny Shute, 149 to 154.

*Uganda be kidding. At the Kampala Golf Club,
hippopotamus footprints aren't a hazard. The hippos
themselves, however, definitely are.*

A local rule at Kampala Golf Club in Uganda
allows free relief from hippopotamus footprints.
Players are also cautioned to avoid water hazards on
ten of eighteen holes where there's a danger from
crocodiles.

*K*evin Burress's tee shot on the 130-yard 16th
hole at Arroya Del Osa in Albuquerque, New Mexico,
came to rest near a tree. A white duck waddled over
to the ball, nudged it into her nest next to five eggs,
and settled down to defend her domain. Kevin's father
distracted the duck while Kevin retrieved the ball.

A high-flying tee shot by Dave Hickler on the par-three 17th hole at Bangkok Country Club dropped in a water hazard — and bounced out onto the bank. The shot had struck a 12-inch carp, which he found floating next to the ball.

Art May left his tee shot a little short on the 200-yard seventh hole at Pruneridge Golf Club, San Jose, California. The ball was just above a small hole, and as May was about to chip, a gopher popped out, slapped the ball with its tail, and disappeared. The ball rolled onto the green, where May putted in.

A goose sitting by a water hazard on a Massachusetts golf course was hit by a player's shot. The goose waddled over to the ball and kicked it into the water.

*D*uring the 1972 Singapore Open, Jimmy Stewart approached his ball for the second shot on the third hole while a 10-foot-long cobra approached it from the other side. Stewart killed the snake, only to see another emerge from the mouth of the first one. He killed that one, too.

*O*n August 12, 1975, the opening day of grouse season, the first kill was made by eleven-year-old Willie Fraser of Kingussie, Scotland. He got his grouse with a tee shot on the local course.

*D*r. A. Vedros, a veterinarian from Merriam, Kansas, was playing golf at the Broadmoor in Colorado Springs when he noticed a female buffalo in an adjacent field having a hard time calving. He climbed the fence, assisted the birth, cleaned the newborn calf, climbed back over the fence, and finished his round.

*M*olly Whitaker was playing from a bunker at Beachwood, Natal, South Africa, when a large monkey leapt from a bush and grabbed her around the neck. Her caddie hit the monkey with an iron, driving it off.

*P*rentiss Cole of Palo Alto, California, put his 3-wood second shot in the rough on the 465-yard par-four 10th hole at Spyglass Hill Golf Club. A doe emerged from the woods and began nibbling the grass around the ball, clipping it to fairway length. This gave Cole an easy third shot; he struck the pin and had a gimme putt.

*T*he 14th hole at Scunthorpe Golf Club in England is called "The Mallard." On April 24, 1965, Jim Tollan's drive on that hole struck and killed a female mallard in flight. The mallard was stuffed and is now on display in the clubhouse.

$\mathcal{W}$hile playing in Zimbabwe, Nick Price once thinned a tee shot on a line drive — and struck a nearby bush pig in the rear end. His ball was not recovered.

$\mathcal{A}$ land crab crawled out of its hole near the fifth green of the Dania Country Club in Florida and grabbed the ball of Bill Graves. The crab won a tug of war and took the ball back underground.

$\mathcal{T}$homas D. Jones III of Charlotte, North Carolina, topped his tee shot on the par-four 12th hole at Peach Valley Golf Club in Spartanburg, South Carolina. The ball headed into a water hazard but struck a large turtle and bounced 150 yards down the fairway. Jones made par.

$\mathcal{A}$ local rule at the Glen Canyon course in Arizona provides that "if your ball lands within a club length of a rattlesnake, you are allowed to move your ball."

On April 22, 1924, at Duddington, England, a ball became embedded in the back of a sheep. The sheep was chased for a few minutes and the ball fell free.

*Jeff Sluman's playoff hopes washed away when a
suds-soaked spectator plunged into the water
around the TPC's island green.*

During the second hole of a playoff against Sandy Lyle at the 1987 Players Championship, Jeff Sluman was lining up a six-foot putt for birdie and victory on the 17th green when suddenly a spectator jumped into the lake. Sluman's concentration was broken and he missed the putt. Lyle won on the next hole.

The first water hazards were streams (called burns) running across Scottish links on their way to the sea. The featherie ball, used by early golfers, floated so it was possible to play or retrieve them from these hazards.

At the 1973 Masters, J. C. Snead was battling Tommy Aaron. As Snead was about to hit his tee shot on the par-three 12th, Sam Snead, who was watching on a clubhouse television, predicted that his nephew would knock it into Rae's Creek because he had the wrong club. Snead put it into the water and lost to Aaron by a stroke.

*T*he U.S. Open record for highest score on a par-four hole belongs to Ray Ainsley, whose 19 on the 16th hole at Cherry Hills Country Club in 1938 still stands. The California pro hit his second into Little Dry Creek and, as the current carried the ball along, he kept swinging away.

In everyday play, at least three people are known to have fallen into the water around the TPC Ponte Vedra 17th's island green, either while backing up to read the breaks or while running excitedly after sinking a putt.

Curtis Strange might have won the 1985 Masters if he hadn't attempted to play from the edge of Rae's Creek on the 13th hole of the final round. He hit the ball out of the creek only to have it roll back in. Strange scored a 6 on the hole and tied for second in the tournament, two shots behind Bernhard Langer.

Speaking about the 16th hole at Cypress Point, a par three that plays over an inlet of the Pacific Ocean, Jimmy Demaret once said, "The nearest point of relief is Honolulu."

The average green needs 5-7,000 gallons of water a week during growing seaason. The average course might get 150,000 gallons a day, while desert courses have been known to take one million gallons daily.

*A*ugusta National's par-three 12th dampened Tom Weiskopf's spirits and chances at the 1980 Masters. His tee shot found Rae's Creek, and he proceeded to drown pitch after pitch until he eventually got his ball onto the green and putted out for a 13.

*A*t the 1993 Colonial Invitational, Ian Baker-Finch decided he could play a ball that lay just inside the margin of a water hazard rather than take a penalty. Instead of simply removing his shoes and socks and rolling up his pants, the Aussie stripped down to his boxer shorts, waded in, and executed the recovery to a roar of applause.

About 1912, a player qualifying for the Shawnee Invitational for Women took 166 strokes on the 130-yard 16th hole. Her tee shot found the Binniekill River. She went into a boat, rowed by her husband, and tried hitting out as the ball floated downstream (at that time, balls floated in water). She finally hit out a mile and a half away — and landed in the woods.

*Lucky for Bobby Jones that skipping girls led to
a skipping ball at the 1930 U.S. Open.*

In his Grand Slam year of 1930, Bobby Jones had fortune smile upon him at the U.S. Open at Inter-lachen Country Club. In the second round, just as Jones was trying to reach the par-five ninth hole in two, a couple of small girls ran out from the crowd. Jones half-topped his shot, which skipped twice across a lake and finished 30 yards short of the hole. He made birdie and won the Open.

Greg Norman's ball airmailed the 10th green during the 1980 World Match Play at Wentworth, England, hit a spectator in the head, and bounced back on the green. He made par and went on to win by one hole.

*M*ickey Wright recalls that during a tournament in Texas, with a 40-mile-per-hour wind, very hard ground, and perfect timing, she went over the green of a 385-yard hole on her drive.

*D*uring the 1979 English Classic at Belfry Golf Club, Seve Ballesteros hooked his drive on the final hole. It started toward a lagoon, where it bounced off an overturned dinghy on the water's edge and back onto the fairway. From there, Seve made a birdie and won the title.

In the third round of the 1986 PGA Championship, Ben Crenshaw was so disgusted by his approach to the 18th hole at Inverness Club outside Toledo, Ohio, that he tossed his 9-iron into the air. The club came down and hit Crenshaw on the back of the head, leaving a gouge that later required three stitches.

Royalty has its privilege — especially at Royal Wimbledon, where Edward VIII, a 12 handicap, scored a hole-in-one during his year as Club Captain in 1928-1929. The ace came courtesy of five caddies who conspired to see his ball fall into the cup with help on a blind par three.

*D*uring an Italian Open a few years ago, an Italian player three putted a green. A fellow countryman rushed out of the crowd and punched the player on the nose.

*A*t Wentworth Falls, Australia, in 1928, two players in a foursome hit their tee shots to opposite sides of the ninth green. They chipped at the same time; the two balls collided in flight and both dropped into the hole.

*I*mmediately after the gun sounded to start a shotgun event at Highlands Golf Club in Cosmopolis, Washington, Bob LaCroix struck his tee shot on the par-three fifth hole. The ball ricocheted off a tree and into the hole ten seconds after the tournament started.

*N*igel Denham saw his second shot to the 18th green at Moortown, Yorkshire, England, bounce up the steps and into the clubhouse. His ball rolled through an open door, ricocheted off a wall and came to rest in the men's bar. From there he played his shot through an open window to within 12 feet of the flag.

*P*itching to the fifth green at Weston (Massachusetts) Golf Club, Malcolm Russell lodged his ball in a tree. Three days later, while playing the same hole, the ball dropped out at Russell's feet.

*A*rthur Powell sliced his drive on the 265-yard ninth hole at Muskerry, in Northern Ireland. The ball hit the roof of a cottage, bounced back onto the fairway, rolled onto the green, and into the hole.

$\mathcal{A}$s he was sizing up a 15-foot eagle putt on the 280-yard, par-four third hole at Elks Club Golf Club in Rapid City, South Dakota, Mike Williams noticed a ball flying toward him. Hit by Bob Malone, the ball bounced off the foot of Williams' caddie and disappeared in the cup for a hole-in-one. Williams missed a putt.

$\mathcal{K}$y Laffoon once found himself needing to two putt from three feet to win a tournament. He missed his first attempt by three inches. That made him so mad he slammed the putter down on the ball, which jumped two feet in the air and fell into the cup for victory.

*M*ike Reid was in contention for the first time at the 1977 Citrus Open. On the final day, three of his shots struck people — a woman in the back, a child in the knee, and a man sitting in a chair — and each time the ball bounced back onto the green. He tied for ninth.

*B*il Blair parked his golf cart on a hill next to the 11th tee at Valley View Golf Club in New Albany, Indiana. Before he and partner Harry Webb could tee off, they heard a loud bang and watched as the cart rolled down the hill and into a pond. A golfer on the tee behind them hit the accelerator pedal with his shot, releasing the brake. Scuba divers and a tractor recovered all but three of the pair's clubs.

During a round at the Waukewan Golf Club in Meredith, New Hampshire, Bill Hayward's second shot on the 15th hole hit a tree and slammed into a water fountain, turning on the water. "By the time we got there," says partner Charles Beard, "the water was nice and cool."

Playing to the second green at St. Andrews, Horace Hutchinson's ball bounced off the shoulder of R. Kirk, secretary of the Royal & Ancient, and lodged in his breast pocket.

E. D. Anthony, Jr., of West Palm Beach, Florida, hit a shot so high on the third hole at Ocean Reef in Key Largo that the ball struck a small plane about to land at a nearby airport. The plane landed safely; the ball dropped in the rough. Not knowing how to rule, his partners let Anthony hit again without penalty.

A golfer on a public course near San Francisco hit his ball into a grassy overhang on a bunker, where it teetered precariously. While taking a closer look, he sneezed and his dentures fell out, hitting the ball and knocking it into the bunker.

Although Arnie won the 1958 Masters, his caddie nearly walked away with the bigger piece of the first-place check.

After winning his first green jacket and $11,250 at the 1958 Masters, an excited Arnold Palmer paid his caddie. Arnie meant to write a check for $1,400, but mistakenly added an extra zero, giving the caddie a check for $14,000. Palmer realized his error and chased down his caddie before it was too late.

At a tournament in Devon, England, in the late 1930s, professional Cedric Saynor asked an inexperienced caddie, "How far to the green?" The young man thought for a moment then replied, "About two minutes' walk, sir."

*B*obby Jones used to tell this story about a caddie named Cobeigh from Gleneagles, Scotland: If a man he is caddieing for plays well, Cobeigh takes great interest; if he doesn't play well, Cobeigh pays no attention at all. Cobeigh was once caddieing for a man who didn't play very well; by the time they reached the 15th hole, Cobeigh had lost all interest in the game. The man said, "Cobeigh, I think you are the very worst caddie in the world." Cobeigh replied, "Oh, no, sir. That would be too strange a coincidence."

*J*ack Lemmon was lying 10 on a hole at the 1983 Bing Crosby Pro-Am and still had a 35-foot putt remaining. He asked his caddie, "How does this one break?" "Who cares?" the caddie replied.

*S*am Snead, coaching his caddie: "When I ask you what club to use, look the other way and don't answer."

*M*ax Faulkner, winner of the 1951 British Open, had a caddie called "Mad Mac," who said of a tricky putt, "I think it's slightly straight."

Chi Chi Rodriguez, relating his caddie's advice on a putt: "He told me to keep the ball low."

Ray Floyd's former caddie, named Golf Ball, kept notes for each course with distances, hazards, and other information. During the first round at a tournament in Memphis, Floyd missed the first four greens. On the fifth hole, Floyd asked for the yardage and hit a 7-iron 20 yards over the green. Upset, Floyd asked if his notes were for Memphis. Shocked, Golf Ball replied, "Are we in Memphis? I thought we were in Fort Worth."

*G*olf writer and commentator Henry Longhurst told of a London caddie who once said, leaning into the wind at a long par four, "It'll take three damn good shots to get up in two today, sir."

*T*ommy Bolt, known for his angry outbursts, felt his caddie did a poor job at a tournament. After the round, Bolt approached an official for a ruling asking, "I know you can get fined for throwing a club, but I want to know if you can get fined for throwing a caddie."

$\mathcal{L}$ee Trevino's former caddie, Herman Mitchell, took a lot of barbs during a tournament, which helped rev up Trevino. When not playing well Lee would say, "Herman, you can't add." To which Herman replied, "Well, you can't play golf."

$\mathcal{M}$any of golf's early heroes were caddies-turned-players. This impressive bunch boasts many U.S. Open winners, including Walter Hagen, Ben Hogan, Lloyd Mangrum, Byron Nelson, Francis Ouimet, and Gene Sarazen.

*T*he Professional Tour Caddie Association was established in 1981 and is open to caddies who have looped fifteen tournaments in the past two years on the PGA Tour. It has a 38-foot mobile home that follows the Tour. The mobile home has a kitchen, cramped seating for eighteen, and a TV with a satellite dish.

*W*hile breaking in a new caddie, Julius Boros told him to pick up a big divot he had just made. Continuing down the course, Boros reminded the boy to pick up every divot. Around the 14th hole, the caddie was gasping and dragging the bag. "What's wrong?" Boros asked. "Mr. Boros, what do you want me to do with all these divots?"

*D*uring the 1946 U.S. Open at Canterbury Country Club in Cleveland, Byron Nelson's caddie accidentally kicked his ball. The single-stroke penalty put Nelson in a playoff with Lloyd Mangrum, which Mangrum won.

*M*ary, Queen of Scots, made a lasting contribution to golf lingo when she returned to Scotland from France after the death of her first husband, Francis, in 1565. Accompanying the Queen were a crew of cadets, sons of French noblemen who served as pages. She often played the Scottish courses attended by her cadets — which her countrymen pronounced as "caddie."

*F*rom the minutes of the golf committee meeting for April, 1921 at Wykagyl Country Club in New Rochelle, New York: "The [caddie] rates are sixty cents per round, thirty cents for nine holes or less. A member paying an additional fee or gratuity shall be liable to suspension."

*Peter Jacobsen says he'd be better on the court than
Michael Jordan would ever be on the course.*

I'll be playing center for the Bulls before he's on the Tour.

> — *Peter Jacobsen,*
> *on playing golf with Michael Jordan*

*L*ee Trevino, describing his youth: "We had so little to eat that when Mom would throw a bone to the dog, he'd have to call for a fair catch."

*W*hen I was growing up, they had just found radio.

> — *Arnold Palmer, when asked if he watched golf*
> *on television while growing up*

I'm about five inches from being an outstanding golfer. That's the distance my left ear is from my right.

— *Ben Crenshaw*

*P*ressure is playing for ten dollars when you don't have a dime in your pocket.

— *Lee Trevino*

*G*olf and sex are about the only things you can enjoy without being good at [them].

— *Jimmy Demaret*

65

*I*t took me seventeen years to get 3,000 hits. I did it in one afternoon on the golf course.

— *Hank Aaron, all-time home run leader*

*B*ob Hope has a beautiful short game. Unfortunately, it's off the tee.

— *Jimmy Demaret*

I wish my name was Tom Kite.

— *Ian Baker-Finch, on signing a lot of autographs*

*W*inged Foot has the toughest eighteen finishing holes in golf.

> — *Dave Marr, during the 1984 U.S. Open*

*I*f you birdie the 18th, do you win a free game?

> — *John Mahaffey, on the 18th at the TPC Sawgrass*

*A*rnold Palmer is the biggest crowd pleaser since the invention of the portable sanitary facility.

> — *Bob Hope*

I was three over: one over a house, one over a patio, and one over a swimming pool.

> — *George Brett, professional baseball player*

*I*sn't it fun to go out on the course and lie in the sun?

> — *Bob Hope, on cheating*

I call it the Sphinx Links.

> — *Robert Trent Jones, on the course*
> *he designed near the Pyramids*

*T*he safest place would be on the fairway.
— *Joe Garagiola, former baseball player and co-host
of the* Today *show with Bryant Gumbel, on the best
place to stand during a celebrity golf tournament*

I tell myself that Jack Nicklaus probably has a lousy
curve ball.

> — *Bob Walk, professional baseball pitcher,
> on handling frustrations as a golfer*

*I*f I knew what was going through Jack Nicklaus's
head, I would have won this golf tournament.

> — *Tom Weiskopf, on Nicklaus
> winning the 1986 Masters*

I owe everything to golf. Where else could a guy with an IQ like mine make this much money?

— *Hubert Green*

*E*xchange between two television announcers: "Do you think he can get there?" "Yes, if he can hit it far enough."

I just hope we can still get Oreos and Fig Newtons at the turn.

— *Paul Azinger, on Nabisco no longer sponsoring the PGA Tour*

9

The First Time

At the very first Amateur Championship, the USGA ruled that it was dirty pool to let a competitor putt with a cue.

$\mathcal{A}$s early as 1895, the USGA was making equipment rulings. At the first Amateur Championship, Richard Peters was banned from putting with a pool cue.

$\mathcal{T}$he first "round" of golf in the United States occurred on February 22, 1888, on a pasture next to the home of John Reid in Yonkers, New York. Reid and five others played a three-hole layout with just six clubs among them.

The first U.S. Open in 1895 was an afterthought to the first U.S. Amateur. Played the day after the Amateur, this one-day, 36-hole event attracted only eleven contestants.

Only four rookies on the PGA Tour have claimed majors as their first victories. Jack Nicklaus won the U.S. Open in 1962; Jerry Pate won the 1976 U.S. Open; John Daly captured the 1991 PGA Championship; and Ernie Els won the 1994 U.S. Open in a three-way playoff.

$\mathcal{J}$im Benepe, an unknown twenty-four-year-old pro from Wyoming, was excited to receive a sponsor's exemption into the 1988 Western Open — his first PGA Tour event. Benepe made history by becoming the only player to win a PGA tournament in his first attempt.

$\mathcal{T}$he highest score for one hole of the British Open was made at the inaugural event in 1860 at Prestwick, when William Steel shot a 21.

When Jack Nicklaus first broke 70 — while playing with his father one early evening at Scioto — he shot a 34 on the front nine, and came to the 500-yard, par five 18th needing an eagle. Nicklaus landed his 2-iron second shot near a working sprinkler in the middle of the green, 35 feet from the cup. "I remember pulling the sprinkler back, and somehow I holed that putt through all the water," Nicklaus later wrote.

A twenty-year-old South African pro named Gary Player competed in his first British Open at Hoylake in 1956, finishing in fourth place. This was the first of thirty-nine consecutive appearances in the tournament, winning in 1959, 1968, and 1974. Player is the leader in British Opens played.

*I*n 1975, Lee Elder became the first African-American to tee it up at The Masters. Elder missed the cut with scores of 74-78.

*T*he most famous putter in golf, Bobby Jones's Calamity Jane made its debut at the 1923 U.S. Open. After complaining of poor putting, Jones was given the putter by his friend Jim Maiden. The club remained in Jones's bag for all 13 of his major championships.

The first nationally televised golf event was the Tam O'Shanter World Championships in 1953. Chandler Harper was ready to take the $25,000 first prize when Lew Worsham holed out at the par-four final hole with a wedge from 100 yards to win. The next year, the purse was bumped up to $100,000 and millions of viewers wanted to see more of the same.

After leading through fifty-four holes as an amateur in the 1967 U.S. Open, Marty Fleckman turned pro and won the Cajun Classic in his first start as a Tour member. He never again won on the Tour.

77

Gene Sarazen unveiled a new club, the sand wedge, at the 1932 British Open. Hiding it at night, Sarazen used it to win the title.

When Fuzzy Zoeller won the 1979 Masters on his first attempt, he gave most of the credit to Jariah Beard. Having only played one practice round, Zoeller relied on the lifetime Augusta National caddie for club selection and reading all of his putts.

Seve Ballesteros and Ray Floyd paid the price for practicing at The Players Championship.

10

Practice

*F*ollowing a rain delay at the 1987 Players Championship, Seve Ballesteros and his playing partner Ray Floyd warmed up by hitting wood shots from the tee to an adjacent area. They were each penalized two strokes for violating Rule 7-2, which allows only practice putting and chipping on a tee during a round.

In his most competitive years, Jack Nicklaus routinely used practice rounds to prepare for the worst a course had to offer. He would drop balls into the deepest bunkers and the most troublesome lies so he would not be unnerved by them during the tournament.

During a tournament week, a PGA Tour field will use approximately 12,500 practice balls a day. That's nearly 3 million practice balls a season.

In 1936, a young Sam Snead was playing in his first PGA tournament, the Hershey Open, in Hershey, Pennsylvania. His first drive in the practice round sliced so severely that it landed in the middle of the chocolate factory. A second ball suffered the same fate. His third shot found a pond in front of the tee. About to quit, his playing partner, George Fazio, said, "Hit another, son." That ball found the green and Snead shot a 67 — not counting the first three attempts.

*Sam Snead needed either a straighter tee shot
or some whipped cream at the 1936 Hershey Open.*

83

According to the National Golf Foundation, approximately 1,500 commercial driving ranges serve 24.5 million golfers in the United States. By comparison, Japan has more than 4,000 ranges available to its 11.5 million golfers.

After Gary Player claimed to have hit 1,000 practice shots during one tournament week, British golf writer Henry Longhurst asked Player this question: "Whatever do you want to do that for? You know how to play golf already."

The practice range at Muirfield Village in Dublin, Ohio, is considered by many to be the best in the world. The sixteen acre facility is circular so golfers can practice with the wind of their choice.

As a boy, Seve Ballesteros practiced all his shots — even bunker shots — with a 3-iron. He had no choice; it was his only club.

*A*rnold Palmer decided to join the Navy during the Korean War. Instead, he was accepted by the Coast Guard. When transferred to Cleveland, one of his duties was to build a driving range in a supply depot. The admiral liked golf and wanted a place to practice.

*I*f I miss one day's practice, I know it; if I miss two days, the spectators know it; and if I miss three days, the world knows it.

— *Ben Hogan, paraphrasing*
pianist Ignace Paderewski

Arnie's wartime service included keeping the admiral loaded with ammunition — on the practice range.

*T*our regulations limit to one the number of practice balls a professional can play during a practice round. One time, Tommy Bolt dropped a second practice ball and was duly warned he'd be fined twenty-five dollars if he hit it. Bolt called over an official, opened his wallet and said, "Here's $100. I'm going to hit four more."

*Sorry, Arnie (you too, Elvis), but this "King"
was a real one, James II of Scotland,
who teed it up for national honor in the 1680s.*

*K*ing James II of Scotland (ruler from 1685 to 1688) had an argument with two English dukes over who invented golf, Scotland or England. They proposed settling the issue with a match. No fool, the King engaged John Petersone, the best golfer in Edinburgh, as his partner. The Scots whipped the Brits and King James gave Petersone a generous reward to express his gratitude.

*T*o conform to USGA rules, the maximum speed a golf ball can have at impact is 250 feet per second, or 170.45 miles an hour.

*T*he tale that eighteen holes came about because there are eighteen "shots" in a bottle of Scotch whisky is quite humorous, but quite false. Actually, St. Andrews and Prestwick originally had only twelve holes. In fact, the first British Open was decided in one day at thirty-six holes. It wasn't until 1764 that St. Andrews was converted to eighteen holes.

*W*alter Hagen was the first player to enter the clubmaking field when he launched the Walter Hagen Golf Company in 1922.

*T*he only occasion a son succeeded a father as champion of a major was when Old Tom Morris won the 1867 British Open and Young Tom Morris won in 1868. Also noteworthy is that Young Tom Morris is credited with the first recorded hole-in-one during his 1868 victory.

*I*n a full drive by an average adult male golfer, the clubhead swings through the ball at about 90 mph. PGA Tour players range from about 110 to 120 mph; LPGA Tour players, from about 90 to 100 mph.

*Young Tom Morris proved to be a chip off the old block
by winning the British Open the year after his dad.*

A common misconception about putting is that you can put a good roll on the ball immediately. Actually, the ball skids across the surface of the green for about twenty percent of the total distance before friction slows it down enough to start rolling. That's the reason putters have some loft. If they didn't, the ball would be driven into the turf and jump up before going toward the hole.

*I*f you laid golf balls dimple-to-dimple from St. Andrews, Scotland, to Augusta, Georgia, a distance of about 6,100 miles, you would need 230 million balls.

$\mathcal{S}$ome golfers believe they can control impact with their hands. However, it takes about two-thirds of a millisecond for the shock waves to travel up the shaft to the hands. At that point, the ball is a half-inch in flight. It would take another one-fifth of a millisecond before the brain could tell the hands to modify the stroke. By this time, the ball is already 15 yards into its flight.

$\mathcal{T}$here are approximately 200-250 yards of rubber thread inside a typical wound golf ball.

*T*he term "scratch" is derived from 19th-century footraces. The "scratch" was a line scratched in the dirt as the starting line for a race. In some races, some competitors started "from scratch" whereas others received handicaps and started from points farther ahead. Scratch came to mean zero handicap in other sports, most prominently golf.

*G*ene Sarazen once suggested that golf would be more enjoyable if the hole were enlarged to eight inches in diameter, lessening the importance of putting. The idea was tried at a tournament in Florida. The effect on scoring was negligible and the idea stopped there.

*Hoping to make the game easier — and putting
less important — Gene Sarazen thought a big idea
was to enlarge the hole.*

After hitting a shot that rolls a great distance, a golfer will often say that it had a lot of topspin or overspin. This is wrong. The only true topspin shot is a full-blooded top, where the ball dives quickly to the ground. Most likely the ball has been hit with less backspin.

At the USGA's new test facilities in Far Hills, New Jersey, golf balls are tested for conformation to stringent specifications after being warmed in an incubator to 23° Centigrade (or 73° Fahrenheit) for at least six hours.

If he switched from golf to gardening,
Lee Trevino says his tomatoes would come up sliced.

I'm not saying my golf game went bad, but if I grew tomatoes, they'd come up sliced.

— *Lee Trevino*

*H*e hits his divots further than I hit my drives.

— *David Feherty, on John Daly*

I don't go that far on my holidays.

— *Ian Baker-Finch, on John Daly's drives*

*C*hris, the boys are hitting the ball longer now because they're getting more distance.
> — *Byron Nelson to Chris Shenkel on ABC-TV*

*W*e took a mulligan.
> — *Cheryl Kratzert, wife of pro golfer Bill,*
> *on their marriage, divorce, and remarriage*

*D*on't blame me. Blame the foursome ahead of me.
> — *Lawrence Taylor, former football great,*
> *on why he was late for practice*

*W*ould you rather be broke or have money in the bank?

— Ben Hogan, when asked if he would rather be in the lead or a shot behind going into the last round

*B*aseball players quit playing and they play golf. Football players quit, take up golf. What are we supposed to take up when we quit?

— George Archer

I never knew what top golf was like until I turned professional. Then it was too late.

— Steve Melnyk

*M*y wife always said she wanted to marry a millionaire. Well, she made me a millionaire. I used to be a multimillionaire.

— *Chi Chi Rodriguez*

*T*he most dangerous thing I do is drive to the bank. I've got a bad swing, a bad stance, and a bad grip, but my banker loves me.

— *Lee Trevino, on his unorthodox style*

*T*he biggest liar in the world is the golfer who claims he plays the game merely for exercise.

— *Tommy Bolt*

*T*hey ought to be good. They play more golf than we do.
— *Fuzzy Zoeller, after a group of NFL quarterbacks*
got birdies at a tournament

I've gone through more putters than Carters has pills.
— *Tom Watson*

*I*n thirty years, we're going to be in our nineties.
We're going to play three-hole tournaments for
$900,000 and the one who remembers his score wins.
— *Bob Brue, on the Senior Tour*

After the third round of the 1976 Masters, Jack Nicklaus trailed leader Ray Floyd by eight shots; Larry Ziegler was nine back in third place. A reporter asked Ziegler what he had to shoot the last day to win. "Raymond Floyd," he said.

I want to win here, stand on the 18th green, and say 'I'm going to the World Series.'

— *Larry Nelson, on a tournament*
at Walt Disney World

*A*rnold has more people watching him park the car then we do out on the course.

> — *Lee Trevino, on the enduring popularity*
> *of Arnold Palmer*

I play the game because my sole ambition is to do well enough to give it up.

> — *David Feherty*

*For his first winnings, Jack Nicklaus won the "bear-ly"
sustaining sum of $33.33.*

$\mathcal{J}$ack Nicklaus's pro career certainly didn't get off to the most auspicious start. His first paycheck, for finishing tied for fiftieth at the 1962 L.A. Open, was only $33.33.

$\mathcal{A}$rnold Palmer was the first player to win a million dollars in his career when he finished second at the 1968 PGA Championship, earning $12,500. It took Palmer more than thirteen years to accomplish this feat.

*I*n 1954, Arnold Palmer wanted to buy his future wife, Winnie, an engagement ring but didn't have the money. So he took on what he later termed a "sucker bet" when he first played Pine Valley Golf Club in Clementon, New Jersey, that year: Palmer would win $100 for every stroke he scored under 72; he would pay $100 for every stroke over 80. "I was in love and nothing could scare me," he said. He shot 68. Winnie got her ring.

$\mathcal{A}$t the 1988 Nabisco Championship, Curtis Strange defeated Tom Kite on the second sudden-death playoff hole to become the first player to win more than a million dollars in one year. His victory gave him $1,147,644 in earnings.

$\mathcal{I}$n 1994, Fuzzy Zoeller became the only player to win more than a million dollars in one season without a victory. He won $1,016,804 by finishing second five times.

*G*reg Norman tops the career money list. Through the 1995 Tour Championship, Norman has amassed a total of $9,592,829.

*A*fter winning the 1975 Pleasant Valley Classic, Roger Maltbie took his $40,000 check to a bar to celebrate. When he awoke the next morning, the check was nowhere to be found. He had to stop payment on the check.

In 1930, the richest tournament in golf was the Agua Caliente Open, in Tijuana, Mexico, offering a total prize of $25,000 with the winner receiving $10,000. Gene Sarazen won the event and needed a wheelbarrow to carry off his winnings.

When Sam Snead won the first Bing Crosby National Pro-Am, held at Rancho Sante Fe Country Club near San Diego in 1937, Crosby presented him with the first place check for $500. Somewhat flustered, Snead said seriously, "If it's all the same to you, Mr. Crosby, I'd rather have the cash."

*I*t's the first job he's had since I married him.
> — *Jeanne Weiskopf, on her husband Tom's*
> *new career as a golf course architect*

*W*hen Lee Trevino won $1,190,518 in 1990, he became the first player to top the million-dollar mark in one season on the Senior Tour. That year, Trevino earned more than Greg Norman, who led the PGA Tour with $1,165,477. Of his record-setting season, Trevino quipped, "It's like being named MVP and leading in batting average, runs batted in, and home runs."

In 1957, Gary Player told his future wife, Vivienne Verwey, that they could get married if he won a tournament in Melbourne, Australia, that had a first prize of $14,000. He did, and they did.

Curtis Strange had a comeback year in 1987, but not in the usual sense. He elevated his earnings from the year before by moving from $688,241 to nearly a million dollars, the largest single-year increase in the history of the PGA Tour.

*B*yron Nelson won $63,335 in 1945 — fourteen and a half percent of the total purse that year. If a player were to win the same percentage of money in 1996, he would take home more than $11 million.

*H*orace Rawlings, an Englishman, took home $150 of the $335 purse for winning at the first U.S. Open Championship. At Shinnecock Hills Golf Club in 1995, Corey Pavin won $350,000 from the total purse of $2,000,000.

When the British Open first went to Muirfield in 1892, the people of Musselburgh, where it had been held previously, planned to stage their own tournament on the same days and with a £100 prize, five times the Open purse. The Open then increased its prize to £110, and the tournaments wound up being played in successive weeks. The Open was won by Harold Hilton, an amateur, and the Honourable Company of Golfers, rather than give the prize to a low professional, kept the first prize of £35.

The first 19th hole — at St. Andrew's Golf Club outside New York — served the same purpose present ones do: eating, drinking, and napping.

*I*n 1892, the 19th hole at St. Andrew's Golf Club, Yonkers, New York, didn't have a bar; in fact, it didn't even have a roof. The 19th hole was an apple tree where members would hang their coats, lunches, and wicker baskets containing Scotland's other gift in the branches. A wide wooden bench around the trunk could accommodate most of the thirteen members of the Apple Tree Gang.

*S*outh Carolina Golf Club in Charleston was the first golf club in America, dating from 1786. The club closed its doors in the early 19th century and bears ancestral roots to the current Country Club of Charleston.

Chicago Golf Club had the first 18-hole golf course
in the United States. Designed by Charles Blair
Macdonald, a chronic slicer, the holes were routed
clockwise. Any hooked shot landed in a cornfield,
from which several strokes were required to extricate
the ball. Consequently, the first out-of-bounds stakes
were placed down the left side, and players could
retee with a penalty without playing from the field.

The first clubhouse in America was located at Shinnecock Hills in Southampton, New York. It was
designed by Stanford White in 1892.

Shinnecock's original 12-hole course was built in 1891. Designed by Willie Dunn, a professional from Scotland, more than 150 workers from the nearby Shinnecock Indian reservation provided the labor for its construction. This course soon became so crowded that an additional nine holes were added — for use by the women members.

Andrew Carnegie was a member of St. Andrew's and built a house next to the course. He spent much of his time there and this was where he negotiated many of his business transactions, including the founding of U.S. Steel.

*T*he 1896 U.S. Open was played at Shinnecock. Among the entrants were John Shippen, an African-American widely regarded as the first American-born professional, and Oscar Bunn, a Shinnecock Indian. Many of the other contestants protested to boycott the competition. Theodore Havemeyer, president of the USGA, told the protesters, "We will play the Open with you or without you." They played. Shippen finished fifth.

*I*n the 1889 British Open at Musselburgh, Andrew Kirkaldy's amateur partner scored an ace on the last hole — when it was too dark to see the green.

Shinnecock was the first incorporated club in the United States. In 1891, forty-four members — both men and women — bought up to ten shares for $100 each. Three years later, Shinnecock had a waiting list — the first club to have one.

When The Country Club in Brookline, Massachusetts, was founded in 1882, the main activity was horse racing. Golf's arrival in 1892 caused problems, as the holes cut through the horse track and paths. One of the biggest complaints of the golfers was hoof prints on the greens.

*In the early days of The Country Club, it was hoofers
versus hookers. Eventually, the golfers won out.*

*A*s a student at Cornell University, Robert Trent Jones created his own major, Golf Architecture. Along with classes in landscape architecture, agronomy, hydraulics, horticulture, and turfgrass science, he studied the classics, philosophy, and history. After graduating, the young Jones was so learned and well respected that even successful golf course architects, such as A. W. Tillinghast, sought him out for advice.

*T*he rocks that line the water hazards at PGA West in Palm Desert, California, were trucked in from over a hundred miles away. Once they arrived, they were stained red to fool golfers into thinking they were chiseled from the nearby Santa Rosa Mountains.

$\mathcal{S}$am Snead's first impression of the Old Course at St. Andrews was not a good one. Looking out the window of a train while traveling to the 1946 British Open there, he asked, "What is this old, abandoned golf course?" Despite this inauspicious introduction, Snead went on to win the championship.

$\mathcal{A}$t the 1953 Crosby (now the AT & T Pebble Beach National Pro-Am), Porky Oliver played Cypress Point's 233-yard, par-three 16th hole — which demands a carry over a Pacific Ocean inlet — into a 50 mph wind. Oliver's first five shots landed in an ice plant. He took three hacks to get the ball onto the green and two putted for a 16.

$\mathcal{B}$uilt in 1854, the clubhouse at Augusta National Golf Club is said to be the first cement house ever constructed in the South. The windows were built so the master could overlook and observe workers in the fields that now make up the famous golf course.

$\mathcal{I}$n the early 1800s, golfers removed sand from the hole just finished to fashion a tee for the next hole. This meant the cup grew larger as the day wore on. Finally, a sandbox was provided for golfers and teeing ground was moved away from the previous green. This preserved the size of the hole until the invention of the hole cutter in 1849.

*Lee Trevino wanted to cut a deal with the R & A
to cash in on lost balls.*

Golf Balls

At the 1983 British Open at Royal Birkdale, the Royal & Ancient drew fire from many players over the brutal rough, except from Lee Trevino, who said, "I have a deal with Keith MacKenzie [former R & A secretary]. After the Open, when they cut this grass, I want to split the take when they find all these balls."

*T*itleist, the country's largest seller of golf balls, began in 1932 in a dentist's office. Phil Young, an amateur golfer and owner of a rubber-parts company, was frustrated with the erratic performance of his golf balls. He and his golf partner, a dentist, X-rayed them. This revealed that the centers were asymmetrical and different sizes. Young and an engineer then created a way of making consistently wound rubber balls.

*T*he earliest golf balls, probably beechwood, gave way to featheries as early as the 15th century when it became the single most popular ball choice for more than 400 years. Making a featherie ball was a laborious process — a top-hat-full of boiled feathers was packed into a leather outer shell with an awl, hammered until round, and then painted. Makers could produce only three or four balls a day, making them so valuable that, in 1637, a teenage boy was hanged in Banff, Scotland, for stealing featheries.

*T*he gutta percha ball, or "guttie," a solid ball made from the gum of a Malaysian tree, appeared in 1845 and was formed by rolling the heated gum into a sphere. Golfers, accustomed to paying as much as five shillings (about forty-five cents) per featherie, were able to purchase a guttie for one shilling. A top guttie maker could turn out as many as 15 balls a day.

*O*n a cold day — below 40° Fahrenheit — a wound ball is slower by about 10 feet per second; a two-piece ball loses about five feet per second.

131

The guttie was not warmly welcomed by the featherie ball manufacturers, especially Allan Robertson, who bought all the gutties in St. Andrews and burned them. Old Tom Morris, Robertson's apprentice at the time, swore allegiance to Robertson and the featherie, but had to break his vow when he ran out of balls and borrowed a guttie. Robertson and Morris parted company.

The most ill-fated gutta ball was the Vardon Flyer. In 1900, Harry Vardon toured America promoting his ball, made by Spalding, becoming the first athlete to sign an endorsement contract. He won the U.S. Open that year using his Flyer, but the Haskell was gaining in popularity. By 1903, Spalding was promoting its own rubber ball, the "Wizard," and in 1909, a catalog offered the obsolete Vardon Flyer as "the best solid gutta ball ever made, excellent for practice."

*I*n 1906, Goodrich introduced the "Pneumatic," a ball with a rubber core filled with compressed air. The Pneumatic had a tendency to explode in flight or even in your pocket. Willie Dunn, using the ball in an exhibition at St. Andrews, sliced into the gallery. It exploded in midair, injuring a spectator. Goodrich, realizing its danger, retired the ball.

*A*s of June 1, 1996, there were 1500 makes and models of golf balls approved for play by the USGA.

*As Willie Dunn learned, the Pneumatic ball, circa 1906,
gave new meaning to the term "explosion shot."*

Since 1981, each golf ball on the USGA's "List of Conforming Golf Balls" has had to pass five requirements: proper weight, size, spherical symmetry, initial velocity (speed immediately after impact), and overall distance (maximum yardage limit, carry plus roll).

Among the substances rumored to fill a golf ball's center over the years have been blood, tapioca, battery acid, and castor oil.

*A*fter Marie Curie published her 1910 treatise on radium, the Worthington Golf Ball Company produced a short-lived fad: the "Radio," a ball with a radium-enlivened core.

*I*n the index to the 1996 Official Rules of Golf, there are ninety-nine separate references to "the ball."

*I*n 1995, approximately 450 million golf balls were sold in the U.S., almost two for every American man, woman, and child.

*A*fter the patent for the first wound rubber ball expired in 1915, the USGA experimented with size and weight of balls. In 1923, limits were set at no more than 1.55 ounces and no less than 1.68 inches. The "balloon ball" that resulted was too light to hold the line while in flight or on the green. In 1932, the current standards were set at 1.62 ounces and 1.68 inches.

*I*n cold weather, gutties became brittle and easily flew apart on contact. The Rules were amended allowing players to drop another ball next to the largest remaining fragment.

*The Iceman commandeth: Clifford Roberts gave the cold
shoulder to flowers that started blooming too early.*

Augusta National takes pride in its azaleas. One year, they were blooming too early, so Clifford Roberts ordered workers to pack ice around the plants' roots in an effort to slow down Mother Nature.

Clifford Roberts, the first Masters tournament chairman, wanted to name the inaugural event in 1934 "The Masters" but Bobby Jones thought it too presumptuous. They called it the Augusta National Invitational Tournament, but it became known as The Masters the following year.

At the trophy presentation for the Masters, the previous year's champion helps the new winner into his green jacket. This was a problem in 1966 when Jack Nicklaus became the first player to capture back-to-back titles. After a moment Bobby Jones said, "We have decided you will just have to put the green jacket on yourself."

On the first tee at the 1968 Masters, Marty Fleck-man hit a huge slice that landed in a parking lot 75 yards from the fairway. He asked an official if he should play a provisional ball. The official replied, "I don't know. Nobody's ever hit it there before."

The Masters is the only major in which no player has broken 70 in all four rounds the same year. Three players have three sub-70 rounds with a 70 in the other: Ben Hogan in 1953, Arnold Palmer in 1964, and Fred Couples in 1992 — all winners those years.

*O*nly two players with at least ten starts have made the cut at The Masters each time. Nick Faldo is 12 for 12 with two wins and Fred Couples is 11 for 11 with one green jacket.

*I*n October 1894, St. Andrew's Golf Club in New York held an open championship to determine the best professional golfer in America. Four professionals competed at match play — Willie Dunn, W. F. Davis, Willie Campbell, and Samuel Tucker. Dunn defeated Campbell 2-up in the final.

*T*he U.S. Open field originally played 36 holes in two days. In 1926, the USGA switched to a three-day format — 18 holes the first two days and a 36-hole final day. But in 1965, Sunday was a leisurely 18-hole round. Influenced greatly by Ken Venturi's dramatic 8½ hour travail in 100-degree heat at Congressional Golf Club in 1964, the USGA decided the Open was to be a test of skill, not endurance, and switched to four days of 18 holes.

The U.S. Open, more than any other major, tends to go into overtime. Of the 96 Opens played, 31 have gone past regulation. Compare that with 11 of 57 Masters, 12 of 125 British Opens, and 8 of 38 PGA Championships (at stroke play).

The only major to slip by Sam Snead was the U.S. Open. But he came close — many times. Between 1937 and 1977, Snead finished second four times, third once, fifth twice, and in the top ten another five times.

*I*n 1947, hometown boy Chick Harbert appeared to have the advantage over Jim Ferrier at the PGA Championship at Plum Hollow Country Club in Detroit. Worried about the partisan gallery, Ferrier hired policemen to guard each side of the fairway so his ball wouldn't be tampered with or kicked into the rough. Ferrier won the championship.

*Jim Ferrier needed police protection to help him nab
the 1947 PGA Championship.*

147

The oldest U.S. Open champion, Hale Irwin, won in 1990 when he was forty-five years, fifteen days old. The youngest, John J. McDermott (also the first homegrown victor), won in 1911 when he was nineteen years, ten months, and fourteen days old.

After shooting a 77 in the first round of the 1974 U.S. Open at Winged Foot, Homero Blancas was asked, "Didn't you have any uphill putts?" to which Blancas replied, "Yeah, after each of my downhill putts."

*G*ary Player won the 1965 U.S. Open at Bellerive Country Club, but lost money in the process. First prize was $26,000, but at the trophy presentation Player donated $5,000 to cancer research and another $20,000 to the USGA for junior golf. After paying his caddie $2,000 for the week, he was in the red $1,000.

*I*n 1935, Jimmy Demaret sent a letter to the USGA's New York City office on East 42nd Street which read, "Enter me Open. Jim." It was his entry for that year's U.S. Open, since no official forms existed before 1936. What was unusual was that Demaret had sent the missive airmail from Herald Square (34th Street and 6th Avenue), a distance of eleven blocks.

$\mathcal{J}$ack Nicklaus has competed in the most consecutive U.S. Opens with forty appearances between 1957 and 1991. He also owns the record for making the most Open cuts, thirty-three.

$\mathcal{S}$iwanoy Country Club in Bronxville, New York, was the site of the first PGA Championship in 1916. Jim Barnes won $500, a medal, and temporary possession of the Wanamaker Trophy, donated by Rodman Wanamaker, heir to a department store fortune.

*T*he PGA Championship was a match play even from 1916 until 1957. Under this format, Walter Hagen won a record five times — including four times in a row from 1924 to 1927, when he beat twenty-two consecutive opponents.

*S*urviving stifling heat at San Antonio's Pecan Valley Country Club in 1968, forty-eight-year-old Julius Boros became the oldest victor of the PGA Championships.

It's tough to triumph two years in a row at the PGA, which produced no repeat champions between 1937 and 1995. The last back-to-back champion was Denny Shute, 1936-1937.

The longest putt holed in a major championship was 110 feet by Nick Price in the 1992 U.S. PGA Championships. A putt of more than 100 feet was also reportedly made by Bobby Jones on the fifth green at St. Andrews during the 1927 British Open.

*T*he only brothers to win the PGA Championship were Lionel and Jay Herbert. Lionel won the last match-play PGA Championship (1957), beating Dow Finsterwald in the final. Jay overcame a devastating double-bogey in the last round at Firestone Country Club in 1960 to nose out Ferrier.

*F*uzzy Zoeller is the only player to win playoffs in majors under two different formats. He beat Tom Watson and Ed Sneed in sudden death in the 1979 Masters, and outdueled Norman 67-75 over 18 holes at the 1984 U.S. Open.

When Hillcrest Country Club in Los Angeles hosted the 1929 PGA Championship, tournament officials decided to add a touch of Hollywood to the event: Fay Wray, a glamour girl of the day — she is best known for starring opposite the ape in "King Kong" — announced players on the first tee. All went well until she called Walter Hagen the "Opium Champion of Great Britain."

At the age of sixty, Sam Snead finished only three shots behind winner Gary Player in the 1972 PGA at Oakland Hills Country Club.

*T*he worst playoff record on the PGA Tour belongs to Ben Crenshaw, whose lifetime record is 0-8.

*T*he British Open's first thirty-four Championships were played in Scotland. In 1894, the Open came to English soil for the first time at Royal St. George's — a long and difficult test. It produced the highest winning score in Open history, a 326.

The first live telecast in Britain of the Open in 1957 caused quite a stir. Viewers watched as the winner, Bobby Locke, failed to properly replace his ball on the last green. The R & A realized Locke's error hours after reviewing the film, but allowed his three-shot victory to stand. Had Locke been disqualified, runner-up Peter Thomson would have won his fourth straight championship. Thomson won again the next year.

*Y*oung Tom Morris so truly exemplified the spirit of the British Open that when he won the tournament for the third time in a row in 1870, officials let him keep the prized Challenge Belt. The following year, a new prize was offered — the silver claret jug still in use today.

*T*he PGA is the only major title to have eluded Arnold Palmer. In 1964 at Columbus Country Club, he became the first to shoot four sub-70 rounds in a major, but this feat only earned him one of his three runner-up finishes.

*Young Tom Morris fought successfully three times for the
Challenge Belt, finally winning it for keeps.*

*N*ew Zealander Bob Charles is the only left-hander to win the British Open (1963) or any other major championship.

*T*he minuscule eighth green at Royal Troon, dubbed "The Postage Stamp" by British Open champion Willie Park, never saw seventy-one-year-old Gene Sarazen's putter in two rounds of the 1973 British Open. Miraculously, he holed a tee shot and a bunker shot, playing the hole three under par.

*F*ormerly of St. Andrews, Jock Hutchinson was the first American citizen to win the British Open in 1921. The next year, Walter Hagen became the first American-born player to claim the crown.

*B*ob Martin won the 1876 British Open by default. He tied with David Strath, who had been accused of breaking the rules by hitting into players on the Road Hole green during his last round. When the championship committee refused to rule on the matter until after the playoff, Strath refused to play further.

*T*he first British Open champion to record three rounds under 70 was Arnold Palmer in 1962 at Troon (71-69-67-69-276). Palmer won by six strokes over Ken Nagle.

*G*reg Norman shares with Craig Wood the dubious honor of having lost all four majors in playoffs. The 1984 U.S. Open went to Fuzzy Zoeller, the 1987 Masters to Larry Mize, the 1989 British Open to Mark Calcavecchia, and the 1993 PGA to Paul Azinger.

17

Course
Stories
Part 2

Ben Crenshaw with TPC at Sawgrass designer Darth Vader.

*F*ew courses have opened to such harsh reviews as the TPC at Sawgrass. Ben Crenshaw suggested Darth Vader, not Pete Dye, had designed it. John Mahaffey questioned its ultra-modern design by openly wondering, "If you birdie the 18th, do you win a free game?" Another venomous remark issued from J. C. Snead, who said forthrightly, "This course is ninety percent horse manure and ten percent luck."

*T*here is a triple green designed by Jack Snyder at Cave Creek in Arizona. It's the green for the first, fifth, and 10th holes.

The longest par four is the 513-yard 10th on Royal Johannesburg (South Africa) Golf Club's East Course. Since the course is at an elevation of 6,000 feet and has hard, dry fairways, the ball carries about fifteen percent farther than normal and rolls much more.

The longest hole in the United States is the 841-yard 12th hole at Meadow Farm Golf Club in Locust Grove, Virginia. It plays to a par six.

*T*he USGA recommends that, for men, par-three holes be no longer than 250 yards; par fours, up to 470; and par fives, 471 and longer. For women, it recommends par three be no longer than 210 yards; par fours, up to 400; par fives up to 575; and par sixes, 576 and longer. The USGA adds that allowances should be made for the lay of the land, any difficult or unusual conditions, and the severity of hazards.

*G*eorge Thomas sunk a bunker in the middle of the sixth green at Riviera Country Club in Los Angeles.

*T*he longest hole in the world is the par-seven, 964-yard seventh hole at Satsuki Golf Club in Sano, Japan.

*T*he world's longest par three is the 277-yard seventh at the International Golf Club in Bolton, Massachusetts.

*T*he longest par five is the 710-yard 17th hole at Palmira Golf Club in St. John, Indiana. The hole is relatively flat and straight with no difficult hazards.

$\mathcal{A}$t the TPC at Sawgrass, Pete Dye originally employed small herds of goats to devour the weedy growth in the rough as they do in parts of Ireland. Dye and the developers forgot one crucial thing — Ireland doesn't have alligators, which ate the goats. The TPC needed to buy some mowers.

$\mathcal{A}$t the 18th green at Carmel Valley Ranch in California, you could encounter a 90-yard putt that must clamber up five levels to reach the pin. Pete Dye made a five-tiered green that cascades from where he thought the green should be to where the developer wanted it.

When Oakmont opened in 1904, there were 220 bunkers — better than a dozen per hole. To make the shallow bunkers more difficult, greenkeeper Emil Loeffler concocted a heavy rake with wide teeth that left deep furrows in the thick brown sand. In the 1960s that sand was replaced, many of the bunkers filled in, and the special rake was eliminated.

Pebble Beach and Cypress Point made you want to play golf, they're such interesting and enjoyable lay-outs. Spyglass Hill — that's different; that makes you want to go fishing.

— *Jack Nicklaus*

*I*n the 1980s, as the environmental movement swept the globe, biodegradable tees were introduced. Designed to save trees, dissolve in the earth, and not dull mower blades, the early models tended to dissolve in the golfer's pocket.

*T*he first years of Alice and Pete Dye's design business were low-budget. For one project, Alice propagated the bentgrass in their yard and transported it to the site in the trunk of Pete's car.

After architect Robert Trent Jones reshaped the par-three fourth hole of Baltusrol's Lower course before the 1954 U.S. Open, many members complained that it was too difficult. So Jones and three club officials went to play the hole. Jones hit last and scored an ace. "As you can see, gentlemen," he said, "this hole is not too tough."

*S*peaking to course architect Robert Trent Jones, Jimmy Demaret quipped: "I saw a course you'd really like. On the first tee you drop a ball over your left shoulder."

*W*hen speaking of the rough at the 1974 U.S. Open at Winged Foot, Hubert Green said to Lanny Wadkins "You couldn't have had too bad a lie. I could still see your knees."

The rough was so high at the 1974 Open at Winged Foot,
Lanny Wadkins lost sight of his legs.

*A*rthur Hills designed a par-three hole under the approach to McCarran Airport in Las Vegas with four tee areas shaped like a spade, a heart, a club, and a diamond.

*B*e careful on Tom Fazio's long uphill par-five finishing hole at Barton Creek Club in Austin, Texas — you can lose your ball in a natural cave just short of the green.

18

Mr.
President

*Ike allowed his opponent only one of two options —
poison ivy or a penalty stroke.*

*D*wight Eisenhower was a stickler for the Rules. Ike was playing with a member of the House of Representatives at Burning Tree when the congressman sliced his tee shot into the center of an ominous cluster of poison ivy. "I can't play that lie," moaned the congressman. "Yes, by golly, you can," said Ike. "If you get poisoned, I'll have Doc Snyder treat you." Major General Howard Snyder was the president's personal physician.

*W*hen President Dwight Eisenhower would putt on the White House lawn, squirrels often would interfere with his practice. Ike had them trapped and removed.

*P*resident Warren Harding hated to wait and insisted on driving and chasing his ball before his playing partners hit. Sportswriter Ring Lardner, who was unaware of the president's impatience, let loose a low screamer one day that missed Harding's head by about an inch. "Well," said Lardner, "I tried my level best to make [Calvin] Coolidge president."

*G*olf runs in George Bush's family. His maternal grandfather, George Walker, was president of the USGA in 1920 and donated the Walker Cup in 1932.

Warren Harding once asked Walter Hagen if there was any favor the president could do for him. Hagen replied, "I have a reputation for being late to my golf matches, and I sometimes drive too fast. One of those deputy Secret Service badges you sometimes give out would do me a heap of good with the speed cops." Hagen got the badge.

Gerald Ford often played during his term in office. A long hitter, Ford outdrove Palmer and Gary Player in the first tee during the inauguration of the PGA/World Golf Hall of Fame at Pinehurst, North Carolina, in 1974. His poke measured 275 yards.

William Howard Taft was the first president to
take golf seriously, despite his massive stature. He
was 6 feet tall and weighed nearly 350 pounds.
Usually scoring below 100, he once took twelve
blows to get out of a bunker. Witnessed by the
Secret Service, Taft faithfully recorded each stroke.

As president, Jimmy Carter didn't play golf. However, he was an avid fan of Putt-Putt, a more serious
version of miniature golf. He was introduced to the
game in 1966 while campaigning, unsuccessfully, for
the Georgia governorship.

Dwight Eisenhower and Arnold Palmer grew to be good friends after playing in many exhibitions. On September 10, 1966, the doorbell rang at Palmer's home in Latrobe, Pennsylvania. Winnie, Arnold's wife, said, "Answer it, Arnie, it's the TV repairman." When he did, there stood Ike, carrying a farm scene he had painted for Arnie's birthday.

Presidents since Nixon have given out signature-stamped golf balls as souvenirs. Since Jimmy Carter did not play golf, his golf balls were stamped with the presidential seal.

John F. Kennedy was playing with aide Chris Dunphy at Seminole Golf Club when he hit an approach shot to three feet. "Gimme?" asked Kennedy. "No," said Dunphy, "that's a character builder." "Okay," replied Kennedy, who looked at his watch and said he had to hurry to lunch with Mortimer Kaplan, commissioner of the IRS. Immediately, Dunphy knocked the ball away, saying "It's good."

In 1991, George Bush made an addition to the White House: a 1,500-square-foot, nine-hole practice green. The $20,000 green, with its special artificial turf, graces the front lawn of the White House.

Gerald Ford has had more professional help with his game than any other president. He has received swing tips from Jack Nicklaus and Tom Watson. Hale Irwin helped him with his tendency to hook irons and Dave Stockton coached him on his chipping and putting.

Richard Nixon said of golf: "By the time you get dressed, drive out there, play 18 holes and come home, you've blown seven hours. There are better things you can do with your time."

Index